# In-Plant Action I

Creating Sustainable Change through Empowerment

**ISBN:** 978-0956082237

First Published November 2008

ALA INTERNATIONAL PUBLISHING

Lutterworth.  England - alapub@ala-international.com

Email - george.boulden@ala-international.com

Web site - www.ala-international.com

Ed 10 January 2023

# Contents

# Acknowledgements

I would like to begin by acknowledging the great debt of gratitude I owe to Professor Reginald (Reg) Revans, the founder of the Action Learning movement. We met in 1974 when he was planning his first Action Learning programme in GEC. At the time of our first meeting I had recently transferred from line management into a management development role. I was very aware that mature managers did not respond well to 'teaching' and was searching for ways of creating learning opportunities. Over lunch Reg shared his ideas with me and I was sold; thirty-five years later I am still a convinced action learner. He introduced me to Alan Lawlor who pioneered Own Job Action Learning in the West Midlands and the three of us created Action Learning Associates (ALA) Intentional in 1980 to promote the application of Action Learning. My relationship with Reg continued until his death in 2003.

I would like to acknowledge my good friends Malcolm Farnsworth, John Cooper and Professor Steve Iman of Cal Poly Pomona CA.

Malcolm, who as Principal of the Marconi Staff Development Centre in Chelmsford, gave me the chance of a new career in management development which I have pursued for a very stimulating thirty-five years.

John, who I worked with at The Dunchurch College of Management, is a natural 'action learner' as anyone who has used or experienced the marvellous business simulations he created will testify and generous to a fault with everything he did. For me John is one of the unsung heroes of Action Learning and deserves to be recognised as such.

Steve for his encouragement and enormous contribution to the publication of the book; without Steve's guiding hand it would probably never have seen the light of day'

Finally I would also like to acknowledge the many hundreds of participants and clients from around the globe who I have learned with and from over the years. It has been a great privilege to know you, thank you all.

George P Boulden – January 2023

# Introduction

*We must be prepared to let go of the past in order to embrace the future (JFK)*

By the 1960's it was clear, to everyone involved that British Industry was, for a variety of reasons, not competitive on the world stage. The Japanese were by then, the World Leaders in productivity. They had 'streamlined' their production processes with such methodologies as JIT and the Kaizen drivers OHE, OEE, TQC etc. Clearly, if we were to compete with them, we needed to emulate them.

The UK Government of the day recognised this need and encouraged management to study these new techniques and to develop their staff through The Industrial Training Act of 1964. This Act required the management of larger companies to introduce a basic minimum level of training for all classes of employee based on the numbers in each class. If the employer met the training goal, he paid nothing, if he exceeded the training goal the Government covered the costs of the additional training if he did less than the requirement he paid the Government for the training which was not done.

For many large companies this became a new source of income. They already had in-house training facilities for groups like Apprentices. They developed these; thousands of people went on training course and companies that managed it well were able to cover their training costs.

In 1972 I joined the teaching staff of the GEC-Marconi Management Training Centre in Chelmsford. This had been opened with a mandate to provide for the management training needs of supervisors and managers in the GEC-Marconi group of 56,000 peop0le.

At that time there was a lot of interest in the difference between teaching and learning.

*Teachers teach students what they believe students need to know.*

*Learners create experiences through which the participants learn what they need to know.*

We were working with experienced managers who we knew would not want to listen to a lot of theory and decided to take the 'learning by doing approach' using simulations, case-studies, projects etc. to create learning experiences. Our programmes were well received and by 1974 we felt we were doing a good job. However all was not well.

As tutors we were responsible for our own programmes which included finding participants. This meant developing relationships with sponsors, usually HR managers, who we met regularly. It was at one of these regular meetings with one of my best clients that I learnt there was a problem. We had completed the pleasantries and I was about to 'pitch' my programme for the semester to one of the HR managers; before I could get going he stopped me. 'Sorry George he said, but we won't be using your training courses anymore'. Why I asked? The answer was simple; he told me that he had just completed a study of labour turnover and discovered that a number of his best younger managers had left the company relatively soon after having attended one of our programmes.

It was clear from the conversation that followed that there was a conflict between the 'participative' message from our training and the strongly parent/child style of management in our learners' companies. Management did not want their people trained. They had to send them on training but all they really wanted from the training was for their participants to have a nice time and come back motivated to work harder not smarter. He never sent anyone else and many other ex-participants I spoke with later confirmed that they had experienced little enthusiasm in their own work places for the introduction of a more participative managing style.

The problem was that we were taking individuals out of their normal environment and introducing them to a participative style of management which we believed, having studied the Japanese approach at first hand, was necessary to achieve any real increase in productivity. What we had not taken into account, or even really thought about, was the influence of their day to day work environment had on how they managed their people.

From this experience I realised that, not only do individuals have values, which determine the 'what' and the 'how' of those things we seek and seek to avoid; organisations also have values which determine their views on what and how things should be done. We were developing individuals in isolation from their work environment. Encouraging them to adopt a more participative style of management in order to improve productivity but this was in direct conflict with the values of their organisations. The message was clear 'Improved productivity through empowerment cannot be achieved solely by training managers; the culture of organisations also needs to change to one which recognises and supports a more participative style of management. It must encourage the use of all of the brains in the organisation, instead of the arms and legs of the many and the brains of the few.

Western management didn't want to understand that the real 'secret' of the Japanese success was their cultural values. For them the goal is the success of the enterprise. For Western management the focus is on what is good for them. The Japanese value their people and their 'style of management' reflects this. As Fujio Cho said 'Many small brains are superior to a few big ones, let's use them. They understand that involvement leads to ownership which creates the commitment that is essential for success. We see such behaviour as a sign of weakness 'managers are there to manage; the workers are there to do what they are told.

When they talk about organisation my Japanese colleagues use the analogy of an Orchestra. Everyone has a part to play, large or small and everyone must play their part perfectly to create the music. To be successful we need management that values all employees for the part they play in the success of the organisation by creating harmony. This, I believe, can only be achieved through participation; but how?

# Action Learning

*We are what we believe*

By 1974 It was clear to me that the real problem in optimising the productivity of organisations was behavioural not technical. The values of organisations, both private and public, reflect the values of their founders. Today's management pass on these values which are normally Parent / Child by promoting people who reflect them; there are those who are brought up to lead and those who follow. This is fine in a world where those at the top know best and those further down do. However, as the world had become more complicated to survive organisations not only need to keep up technically they need to change the way they manage their people. A few large brains may have been good enough to manage an organisation in the fifties but not in the seventies when the brains were on, what used to be, the shop floor. It was also clear that whilst our behaviour is based on What we believe, How behave, is based on our environment. Our development programmes focused on creating a participative environment to optimise performance unfortunately our participants came from and went back to, an autocratic environment.

I was looking for a process that would enable us not only to develop our participants but also enable them to influence the senior managers who sent then to us to:

1. recognise the value of all of their people
2. accept the necessity to involve them
3. accept that changes in management style were also necessary; to enable the organisation prosper Management itself also has to change

By chance, one day, I met Professor Reg Revans and it changed my life. We were both in the GEC Head Office for meetings and met in the lift on our way to find some lunch. GEC Head Office (110,000 employees worldwide) did not provide lunch for visitors! Reg asked me if I knew where to go, I didn't so he took me to a local Pub where he told me about his work with Action Learning and said he was in Stanhope Gate to talk with Sir Arnold Weinstock about running an Action Learning Programme for GEC. I told him about what we were doing in Staff Development and my problem. This opportunity led me, with his help; to participate in the first GEC Action Learning and later to join the teaching staff of the Dunchurch Collage of Management.

During the next four years I had the opportunity to work with my colleagues on a range of Action Learning programmes and meet regular with Alan Lawlor and from time to time with Reg who was busy creating new opportunities for Action Learning. We often talked about how we could we might build on what Reg was doing and by the end of 1979 we were ready to go. I left Dunchurch Collage in the December and in January 1980 we set up Action Learning Associates. Alan was already well established with his Special Own Job programme and to develop programmes through the Government of the time. Reg would continue with what he was doing and helped us where and when we needed him. Note. This turned out to be very helpful in our relationship with people he knew in the International Labour Organisation (ILO) in Geneva leading a number of large projects over next 20 Years. My role was to create and deliver In-Plant Action Learning programmes in my existing client base and develop business opportunities with the ILO.

# The In-Plant Model

*If the mountain won't come to us, we must go to the mountain*

Action Learning, as envisaged by Reg, focused on the development of individual managers. It is a very successful vehicle for individual development because; unlike other more traditional forms of management training it is holistic, encompassing the whole person and reflexive in that it focuses on helping participant's to identifying their development needs. It provides the knowledge, skills and support necessary to succeed.

What we value creates our attitudes; these trigger behaviours which influence our success. Action Learning or Action Reflection Learning as it's more accurately called provides in the one package, the knowledge necessary to understand, the skills we need to do, the experience to be competent and the opportunity to identify and change those values which are inappropriate to what we want to achieve in our lives.

The problem with traditional training programmes, as I discovered in 1974, is that whilst we can successfully take individuals out of their normal environment and develop them, we can't take the impact of environment out of the individual. Our behaviour is influenced by our environment; thus developing individuals in isolation from their 'normal' work environment can be counter- productive. If, for example, a manager learns during a development programme that team working is an effective way of increasing productivity, but finds that team working is unacceptable when he/she returns to their traditionally managed workplace this will cause frustration and in extreme cases the manager may leave the organisation.

To develop an individual we only need the individual because they are the custodians of their own values. With organisations, all employees are at least in part custodians of the organisation's value system; this can only be changed if all employees are, either directly or indirectly involved. This is achieved by empowering employees across the organisation to work together to identify and solve the organisation's knowledge, skills, experience and behavioural problems.

In my experience the main factor impacting organisational performance is not the individuals but the organisational culture which militates against empowerment and thus, productivity. The issue with improving productivity is not that people require training, it is that the culture of traditional organisations needs to change to one which encourages the use all of the brains in the organisation.

The In-Plant version of Action Learning achieves this by going into organisations and empowering employees through involving them, either directly or indirectly in the change process. This creates ownership which leads to commitment. If you are seeking a reliable means of influencing company culture this programme is for you.

In-Plant Action Learning programmes use the structure of traditional action learning programme but there differences:

1.  They involve the whole organisation.

Whilst we as individuals have our own values based on our beliefs organisations both Public and Private sector also have their own value systems. These were created by the founders and are alive well today in the custody of today's people. These values create the environment which in turn dictates the behaviour of the people. If we want the people to change we need to change the values of the organisation.

In-Plant programmes focus on the organisation starting with the top team. The trigger for a programme is usually that management would like to solve some problem or introduce some change. In the main they know what they would like but are looking for help on how best to do it. The traditional approach would be to use a consultancy organisation to produce a proposal which management approve and the consultant runs a project to manage the implementation. The problem with this is that no one is involved and there is no ownership. The In-Plant approach focuses on empowering the people in the organisation to solve their own problems. This is achieved by each set having two projects. One, where they work as a team, is to solve a real problem facing the organisation and the other is to identify and manage personal development needs.

2. Participants manage themselves

During the start-up period of the programme we provide training and support for the sets and encourage them to support each other by rotating the roles of managing meetings and facilitating learning. In addition we provide material support in the form of the 'In-Plant Action Learning Teams – Participants Guide' and regular meeting by the consultants.

3. In-Plant is not a Programme, it's a way of life

The problem for organisations is that whilst most embrace the idea of training their people only technical training, the 'must have' normally survives. What In-Plant demonstrates is the real value of employees can deliver. We encourage clients to see this as something that can be used every day and it's free. How successful are we? Some like it some don't. It all comes back to the values of the organisation!

**Organising the Programme**

Programmes begin with an explanation of the In-Plant process to the top team and their role in it. As part of this introduction we identify the problems they would like to solve through the programme.

**Identifying the Problem**

We start by clarifying whether the problem management is seeking to solve is open or closed. If it is an open problem; one where many different answers are possible, we are seeking to find out WHAT the majority of those involved see as the 'best fit' solution(s). We achieve this by asking all of the people who will be affected by what is decided, what they think would have the greatest impact on improving, for example, performance.

If we have a closed problem; something management has already decided to do, we open this up by asking HOW it should be done and start the programme by involving the people who will be most affected by the changes.

In the WHAT case we engage people by asking them for their opinions about the issues facing the organisation and what they think should be done about them. If for example management believes it needs to become more competitive but not specifically the best way to achieve this we can start the process by asking the employees what they think, using questions like;

*'What could we do to help you to be more productive? '*
*'*
*What stops you doing the best job you can?'*

*'If this was your organisation what would you do to make it more productive?'*

In the HOW case we asked involved employees what they saw as potential issue impacting the planned change.

*'Management plans to double the size of the organisation over the next six months. What do you see as the main issues facing you and how can these be resolved in order to achieve this successfully?'*

Note. In some cases management teams themselves are unsure what they want to achieve. In such circumstances we recommend that management participate in a Business Development Workshop as a pre cursor to clarify how they want the organisation to develop. The outcomes of this workshop are then used as the vehicle for change.

Note. For more information on this please contact us for a copy of our Business Development Workshop programme.

Once we have the right question(s) the next step is to decide how to involve those who will be affected by the proposed changes. Do we involve all employees or specific teams of employees, like supervisors or Divisions /departments etc.? It depends on who will be impacted by the changes. If it's everyone, then everyone needs to be involved which means a company-wide survey. If it's a specific group, like for example supervisors, the questions can be asked in small team meetings etc. The main aim is to involve, if not all of those who will be affected by the actions, then at least a cross section to enable all to identify with the changes.

The data is analysed to identify the key issues that those involved believe need to be resolved in order to ensure the successful implementation of the desired change. This is shared with the management team in the form of a report. The following example shows the results that a company that was planning to double its workforce received from a survey.

*Results of survey of the existing supervisors and specialist personal involved in production. This showed that they felt there were four key issues that needed to be resolved to make the transition successful. These were:*

1. *The line stocking and materials supply systems*
2. *Communication within the plant*
3. *How the flexitime system was working*
4. *Morale and productivity. Note - There were significant absenteeism and labour turnover problems in the plant at this time which made it difficult for the supervisors to achieve production targets.*

Management accepted these issues as being key to success and four of the senior managers agreed to act as 'clients' for the four projects on behalf of the management team. – (See the Chapter on Case studies for the complete case)

**Writing the TOR's**

We start by getting agreement with senior management on which of the issues raised by the employees they see as key to what they are seeking to achieve. Once the key issues have been agreed members of the senior team are asked to select an issue they feel strongly about. They then become the 'client' to the Action Learning teams that will be created to work on that specific project and are asked to create Terms of Reference for the project teams. The following example shows how this is done:

---

**PROJECT TERMS OF REFERENCE - EXAMPLE**

Title:   Spares and Maintenance

Purpose: - To create the conditions for 100% on demand availability of production equipment

Client   - Andy Johnson, Production Director

Current Situation - The majority of people who participated in the attitude survey listed lack of repair support as one of their most pressing problems.  They noted that when machines were in functional teams, if one machine broke down its work load could be allocated to another; with the cell system if one machine fails then the whole cell is disrupted. Prior to the reorganisation supervisors were promised that no machine would be 'down' for more than three hours and that sufficient spares would be held to support this objective.

In the event, however, this appears not to have happened.

Activities;  Your task is to investigate this issue to:-

　　1.   Quantify the problem. How big an issue is it really?  What

---

sort of time is lost through maintenance problems? What is it really costing us? Are there any significant differences between maintenance in one area and another and maintenance of one type of equipment and another? Etc.

2. Examine best practice in other organisations. How do they manage their maintenance? How many man-hours are involved? What does it cost? What problems do they have?

3. Make recommendations on what should be done at to resolve the situation.

To ensure commitment to the outcome each member of the management team should have a project. Having written their TOR they share it with other team members and discuss for agreement. When the TOR's are agreed the programme is ready to start.

## Planning the Launch

The Management Team and all of those who will work on the projects need to be invited to the launch meeting. Usually this means all of those who contributed to the problem identification survey, but not always. On occasion we have asked the whole workforce of a thousand or more people for their views on the issues facing the organisation. When we have done this we have ensured that all have the access to our findings and the subsequent projects. In most cases it would not be practical, at least in the first instance, to involve all of these people in the project teams. As a general rule, for the process to work, all senior managers need to be clients, a representative cross section of employees need to work on the solutions and there needs to be seven to eight people in a team. If we have a thousand people with a management team of say ten, we need eighty people to create ten teams. In this case we would recommend that the first line managers form the teams and be responsible for keeping their work teams informed on what was happening. Note. Where an organisation is unionised we recommend that a representative cross section of employee representatives should also be involved.

Once the structure of the programme has been agreed all who participated in the survey can be briefed about the results, the actions management propose to take and how management will keep people informed on what is happening. Note. This is normally done through regular line management briefings. Those who will work in the programme are then invited to a plenary session for briefing. This will usually be held in the evening and has an informal tone, usually starting with a buffet and ending with drinks. The meeting is chaired by the Chief Executive who makes the opening presentation followed by the person responsible for the programme (usually the consultant) who explains the programme for the evening and goes through the report. The management team then present their projects, which are written up on flip charts that are pinned up around the room as they are presented. When all of the projects have been presented the consultant explains that people can now choose the projects they would like to work on and that once this is done people can adjourn to the bar!

Note. The following is an example-briefing note written for a Chief Executive prior to such a meeting.

To: Peter Abernathy – Chief Executive, XXX.

### INTRODUCTION TO ACTION LEARNING TEAM LAUNCH PROGRAMME
### TUESDAY 31ST OCTOBER

*Welcome the team to the meeting.*

*Introduce the fact that you have come in since the start of the programme, but have, with the management team, evaluated what has already been done and feel that this is an ideal vehicle for achieving your goal of improved performance through the development of a participative problem-solving environment at the plant.*

*Tell them that:-*

*The report, which we will be going through later in the session, was discussed in depth at a meeting on the 25th and eight projects were agreed.*

*The seven projects that will be presented this evening are the next stage of the original programme.*

*This is designed to provide an opportunity for you to work together in mixed teams to solve some of the key problems we are currently facing. The projects will be presented by their clients later on.*

*Tell them that the eighth project is one which the management team itself will be working on. This is designed to help us improve our performance; the way we work as a team and the way we manage the business. This project will involve us working together to develop a mission statement for the organisation and to set up goals and controls to measure performance within each function.*

*The overall objective of the management project is to enable us to clarify `where we are going' and to communicate that information more effectively to you. This will enable us to address one of the key issues raised in your comments, of the lack of leadership and direction from management which has obviously had significant impact and morale and therefore performance.*

*Consultant will now explain the programme for this evening and will talk you through the report. Everybody has been given a copy and there will be an opportunity to raise any issues for discussion during his presentation.*

**Getting started - Project Team Workshop**

Programmes normally begin with a half-day workshop attended by all of the project teams where participants are introduced to the concept of working in problem solving teams using the methodology set out in the ALA Manual **In-Plant Action Learning Teams, Participants Guide**. This explains the process and provides some of the basic problem solving tools the teams will need during the project. Workshops normally start with an explanation on how the teams will self-manage the coordination and facilitation of the team meetings with all participants rotating through these roles over time. Participants are presented with a process and skills model for each role. The problem solving exercises are the used to highlight the problem solving process and also to demonstrate how the team leadership and facilitation roles work in practice; see our book on Coordinating and Facilitating Action Learning Teams for more information.

### Investigation and Recommendations Phase – 3 months

In the early programmes we followed Reg's idea that participants in an Action Learning programme should find their own way through the problem solving process and view this as a part of the learning opportunity. So we adopted an unstructured approach, leaving the teams to work through the process with the facilitator acting as their guide. In practice we discovered very quickly that this wasted a great deal of time and was of questionable value from a learning point of view, after all our main focus is on changing the organisation not on developing individuals. We decided that the team's time would be better spent learning about problem solving using a models they are given rather than trying to invent their own thus freeing them to use their energies to learn about working together to solve the problems of their project. We encourage the teams to use the information provided in the Participants Guide referred to in the Introductory Workshop and encourage them to use the Activity Check List to create a work plan with timescales.

Project Investigation Phase - Activity Check List

1. Describe the situation & set objectives
2. Develop a work plan
3. Collect data

4. Analyse the information
5. Define the problem & review objectives
6. Develop alternative solutions
7. Choose one option
8. Risk analysis
9. Write & present a report suggesting recommendations for action

This, essentially practical process, provides the team with a framework for what they have to do in the allotted timescale and a common language for working together. It also provides a structure, which can be used to both keep the team on track and also to report back to the coordinator and consultant at the regular meetings thus enabling the consultant and the coordinator to manage the process.

## Presentation and Feedback Phase – 1 month (Elapsed time)

This is the linking stage between thinking and doing. It is the change-over time when the teams move from the relatively harmless process of investigation into action and the client from supporter to project manager. It involves five distinct steps:

1. Presentation of findings by the project teams
2. Analysis of recommendations by individual clients
3. Agreement amongst clients on courses of action
4. Writing Terms of Reference for the projects
5. Presentation of projects to the individual teams for action

The process usually lasts about three weeks and is the fundamental test of management commitment. If management is serious it will accept and action most of the recommendations. If it is not it try to sweep all the real changes that have been recommended under the carpet.

## The Presentations

Each team will have produced a written report showing what they have done, their findings, the data they have used to reach them and their recommendations. This is normally handed to the client about a week before the presentations, with copies to other members of senior management being made available after the presentation.

The presentations are usually held in an evening and involve all participants, facilitators and clients. This is the opportunity for the teams to formally present their findings to their respective clients and to share what they have done with their fellows. The presentations provide an excellent opportunity to develop participant's presentation skills and are usually done formally, from the front of the room using visual aids like flip charts and data projectors etc.

The teams present in turn, with presentations lasting about half an hour including time for questions. Teams are encouraged to use whatever aids they feel will be useful and generally to make the presentation in the way they think will be most effective. Recording the presentations on CCTV provides an extra learning opportunity, giving the teams the chance to use the recording later to see how they did.

Clients can question their teams during the presentations to clarify issues or to gain understanding, as can other members of the audience; but as the report reflects the team's views and is for a specific client, it is not an open debate; questions are restricted to those concerned with matters requiring clarification. This is particularly important in maintaining team motivation, they have worked more or less hard for three months to produce their recommendations and these should not be judged by instant and usually ill-informed comment in an open forum. Each team will receive feedback from their client after in the feedback session which normally takes place two weeks' later.

The meeting is normally chaired by the consultant as he/she is seen as being impartial and will not become embroiled in debate or allow others to do so. At the end of the proceedings the sponsor thanks the teams for their efforts and the consultant closes the session with a brief statement on what happens next.

Planning the Response and deciding what to implement

Each client is required to feedback his/her reactions to the recommendations. The feedback covers:

1. Overview of the report
2. Actions the clients will take/are taking themselves
3. Recommendations which will not be actioned and why
4. Actions which the client(s) would like the team to implement on their behalf and the results to be achieved

Clients normally have two to three weeks to give their response to the teams.

We recommend that before feeding back to their teams clients meet in plenary and talk through their planned response with their peers. This has the following advantages:

1. Provides an opportunity for discussion before implementation takes place.
2. Ensures that all client focus on something real to implement
3. Avoids duplication or overlap in the implementation phase

This meeting can vary in length from one hour to one day plus, depending on the relationships within the management team and whether they are used to working together. The length of time is not important; the key thing is that each client, his peers, obviously including the sponsor, feels happy with the response and the intended project.

The normal format for these meetings is for each client to go through the project report item by item, telling colleagues how they intend to respond. In organisations where the Chief Executive has strong views, this may take some time, especially if he feels he must express his personal feelings on every point.

Implementation projects can be as simple, as the setting up of a new department to handle goods inwards. Or they may be more complex, as in the case of one Mexican textile company, where all the recommendations on the motivation project pointed towards a lack of organisation and structure. In this case the project to solve the problem was firstly to define the management structure, agree the roles and responsibilities, out of that to identify the training and non-training needs and finally to carry out the training of the personnel involved.

Typical projects have included:

1. Developing completely new management development programmes in a leading National Management Institute
2. Setting up a new internal communication system from management briefings to notice boards in a large UK Brewery
3. Developing and implementing a planned maintenance system in a large joinery Company
4. Designing and implementing a major retraining scheme in a large electronics Company
5. Setting up a system for managing cash flow which produced saving of over £600,000 per annum
6. Putting in a new purchasing system to achieve identified savings of £2M a year

When each client has presented their reactions and the projects have been agreed, the meeting closes and the clients go away to write up their projects. It is useful for the consultant to record what has been agreed, which can be written up and circulated later. The meeting closes when all clients are clear what they are going to say about the things they will act on, the things they will not act on and why and what their projects are going to be.

**Writing the project**

It is important in our experience that the consultant works with the clients to help them write their projects. The project document must be written in such a way that the intended actions and desired outcomes are clear. If possible it should contain time scales, reporting milestones and an outline budget. Once all the projects have been written it is valuable to re-convene the client team for a short meeting so that they can read through their projects to ensure there have been no major changes during the writing.

**Client Feedback**

The next step is for the clients to meet with their teams, to feedback their response to the recommendations and particularly those they would like the team to implement on their behalf. The feedback should be detailed covering all the points raised and the teams should be given copies of the written project brief as their mandate for the implementation phase. If this does not include an activity plan with time scales and budgets then this should be the team's first action. Where the client has laid down the plan and reporting milestones, these are used as the basic reporting points.

These feedback meetings can either be held individually, between the team and its client, or in plenary with all teams, facilitators and clients present. The levels of motivation of both teams and clients usually influence the choice of method. If the teams are strongly motivated and eager to continue and the clients are supportive and keen to get things done, individual client, team feedback will be most effective. If however there have been problems with the teams, high levels of 'drop out' low motivation etc., if some of the clients are frightened and would rather stop now, a plenary session is the best way to lift the programme up again. This needs to be led by the sponsor who with the help of the external consultant can pull it together. If things are really difficult it may make sense to provide the option to form new teams in the implementation stage. Although in our experience teams have not accepted this, providing the freedom to choose re affirms motivation and commitment. Equally it can be useful, at this stage, to offer the team's specialist help with technical problems.

Once the project has been agreed the clients become project managers and the team is their project team for the duration of the activity.

## Implementation – 3 months (nominal)

The programme is now in the Implementation phase; each team has been asked by their client to implement at least one of their recommendations on his/her behalf. It is very important to recognise that this phase is significantly different from the Investigation and Recommendation phase. Not only because something is being done but also because the project team are actually doing it. It is easy to investigate and make recommendations for others to carry out. It is quite another thing to implement your own recommendations.

The client role also changes from the more 'laissez-faire' approach of the Investigation and Recommendation phase to something much more akin to that of a project manager. The client designates specific objectives, allocates resources lays down time scales, control points etc. The teams are now responsible to their clients for bringing the project to a successful conclusion.

Often this phase will involve the co-opting of 'experts', people with specialist knowledge about technical aspects of the project. This may involve the consultant where he or she has the required skills or other specialists. The teams must be given whatever expert help they need to solve specific problems, what they are doing now is for real. If they have recommended setting up a productivity measurement system but don't have the skills themselves or they need expert advice on how to create a new publicity campaign etc., this help must be provided for the success of the project. Specialist can be recruited, internally if they exist, if not, externally. What the specialist does and the level of involvement depends on the team. They are responsible directly to the client for the successful implementation of the project and it is up to them to use their resources as they see fit to achieve the goal(s).

Teams can also co-opt additional members. These will normally be people who the team feels will be useful in strengthening the team and who are themselves willing to join. A team without a member from finance, implementing a project with financial implications for example, may co-opt someone from the finance department and so on. It is an important part of the co-coordinator/consultant's role to ensure that teams do get the resources necessary to do the job.

**Programme Review and Evaluation**

This is a two part activity consisting of a review of the programme to identify what has/has not been achieved and an evaluation to decide what should be done to integrate the positive benefits of the Action Learning/Team Building experience into the normal operating philosophy of the enterprise.

The review session provides a view of the participant's immediate reaction. If it's been a good programme most people will say so. If they didn't like it no matter what has been achieved, they will also say so. It is really a reward for all the hard work everyone has done. The purpose of the evaluation on the other hand is to provide management with the opportunity to assess the experience and to integrate the positive aspects of the programme into the organisations day-to-day managing philosophy where it can be extended to involve all.

The fundamental problem with most people based performance improvement programmes, quality circles, problems solving teams etc., is that they start with the decision to implement and are evaluated in practice. Managements have to commit themselves to the chosen system before they can learn about its strengths and weaknesses which means that they have to commit before they know if what they have bought is what they want. With an In-Plant programme management learns first, it can choose, based on its own knowledge of applying the philosophy, the most appropriate model for its business. It is this integration of the best of the programme into the organisations managing systems that the past six months have been all about.

The review session is normally run by the participants themselves and involves all clients, facilitators and anyone else who has been part of the programme. The primary objective is to review the programme and evaluate its benefits. What objectives were achieved, what were not and why? It is an opportunity for all involved to share their views about the experience to see what has been learnt from it. Such sessions are usually very open; success and failure are discussed with equal candour, both being seen as providing a learning opportunity. Normally such meeting finish in the bar! Note. In addition the sponsor may wish to obtain more formal feedback which can easily be done using questionnaires after the event.

Evaluation is technically the last stage in the process and the end of the training aspect of the programme. In reality it is the beginning. Until now we have really been concerned with demonstrating a process. Demonstrating that participative problem solving, involving those who have to live with the problems in the process of their solution is the most effective way of solving open-ended problems. That to achieve this management must adopt a more open and involving style. Hopefully we have demonstrated that the approach can and does produce workable solutions to real problems.

It is concerned with where the enterprise goes from here. What has been the real value of the programme? Has it shown itself to be an effective means of solving open-ended problems? What did the sponsor get for his money? Did it really improve performance? What were those achievements? Is the organisation's approach to managing itself more cohesive and organic? Have we really grown the adult? How can the programme be extended, based on the good things we have learnt, to involve everyone? The evaluation and integration process is the key.

The experience can either be evaluated directly by senior management or by a representative team of participants. The senior management team approach is most relevant to smaller organisations. They evaluate the programme and determine what changes should be made in the way the organisation runs. These are then implemented as a policy decision. With larger organisations it is better if the evaluation is to be carried out by a representative team of participants as this creates a climate of ownership of the proposed changes. It is normally run as a three month programme involving one or more participants from each of the action teams. This is a four-stage process:

Stage 1 - Review the experience; identify strengths and weaknesses as they relate the organisations own strengths and weaknesses and produce recommendations on what should be incorporated into the organisation and how this should be done. For example, if the team problem process has been found to be effective and no such system currently exists the team may recommend Quality Circles going down to employee level as a means of incorporating the philosophy in the operating systems of the enterprise. If the communication aspects have been particularly beneficial it may recommend adoption of an integrated team briefing system etc.

Stage 2 - Present findings to senior management, agree recommendations and implementation plan. This will be done informally, as a working party and the meeting will be expected to agree the recommendations during the meeting.

Stage 3 - Present the implementation plans in plenary to whole management team. This presentation is designed to advise the other managers what is happening and will be done by the evaluation team with support of the sponsor.

Stage 4 - Implement

This means creating the structure to make participative problem solving an integral part of future management practice. Our Semi-

Conductor company for example did just that; they used the experience of their In-Plant programme initially as a model for the introduction of their internal problem solving teams and later incorporated the philosophy into the Sequel 5 programme the fore runner of 6 Sigma

# Roles and Responsibilities

The attitudes and behaviour of the key players are crucial to the success of the programme.

**The Sponsor**

The role of the sponsor in In-Plant programmes is significantly different from the role of the sponsor in traditional Action Learning programmes. There the sponsor is often both sponsor and client and is primarily concerned with the development of their participant rather than the management of the programme. With In-Plant programmes the sponsor has decided to use the internal resources of the organisation to implement a desired change so he or she is a key player in all aspects of programme. He / she chooses the projects, selects the clients and the participants in terms of what aspects of the organisation need to be represented to ensure success. He or she leads the launch of the programme and monitors and controls progress through out. This is particularly important in the implementation phase of the programme because it involves change. What is achieved during this phase is heavily dependent on the sponsor. The clients are the direct interface between the sponsor and the teams. If the client is not fully committed to what the team has been asked to implement it is easy him or her 'to kick the ball into the long grass'. Many senior managers don't like participation, don't want change and want any interference in how they manage their functions. For the process to be successful the sponsor must, in Reg's immortal words, know what they want for their organisation, care enough about getting it to have the courage to do what is necessary to make it happen; it's their programme.

The advantage with an In-Plant programme is that the sponsor is not alone; they have the support of the coordinator and the consultant. They know what is actually happening and it is their role to keep the sponsor fully appraised on what is going on and advise on what to do about it. It is the sponsor who must encourage the clients to manage their projects to a successful conclusion. He/she alone can do this. All the coordinator and the consultant can do is ensure that everyone is aware in advance of things that might happen and to flag up any warning signs quickly and encourage the sponsor to keep going.

## The Programme Coordinator

This role does not exist in traditional Action learning programmes because the teams are made up of individuals working on individual projects. The only coordination is of the set meetings and this is normally done by the person running the programme who also facilitates the learning. With In-Plant programmes the activity is within one organisation, not necessarily on the same site and is focused on action(s) which will change the organisation. Both the consultant who is running the programme and the Sponsor need ongoing feedback on how things are progressing and the Senior HR person is in the best position to provide this. He / she understand the need to utilise the power of participation to deliver change successfully and is perfectly placed to monitor the progress of the various projects. They know the projects and attend project performance reviews to obtain up to date information on progress. They will also meet regularly with the clients to get their views on progress and report regularly to the sponsor and consultant on what is happening. Where problems occur they are discussed in the first instance with the sponsor and consultant who will decide the most appropriate action to take. The co-ordinator's main aim is to ensure that everything possible is done to support the successful realisation of the projects.

Our experience shows that the commitment of the HR team is the key to the success of the programme; one needs a champion at the helm. They must be committed to the process and have the influence with the Chief Executive to see the programme through its inevitable up's and down's. The very fabric of the organisational pyramid and all its little fiefdoms are under attack when an In-Plant programme is running. Sacred cows are about to be slaughtered; those with vested interests know this full well and whilst they are officially supportive of the process, unofficially many would like to destroy it. Only a strong HR function can see such change through.

In addition to its management role HR is responsible for 'selling' the idea internally, persuading managers and where appropriate Trades Unions that it's time for a change. They need to be involved in everything, from the decision to start the programme, the data collection, working with the management team to agree projects, who should be involved, organising briefing meetings, helping teams with problems, arranging sandwich lunches and above all acting as a conduit of information to the external consultant.

**The Consultant**

The consultant designs and manages the programme. This starts with the acceptance of the proposal which is followed by data collection and analysis to identify key issues leading to the creation of projects, selection of clients and teams. The consultant is responsible for the development of the structure and the managing the programme, including the organisation and facilitation of team meetings, communication with clients and the sponsor and most importantly the relationship with the programme coordinator. The consultant is fully involved in the pre-launch planning and the Investigation stages of the programme. The degree of involvement of the consultant in the implementation stage of the programme is determined by the participant's level of expertise at this halfway stage. If some facilitators are still working formally with their teams, the consultant will normally continue to work with them. If the consultant is an expert in some area of the projects they may act as a specialist to one or more of the teams. They may even work as a facilitator to one or more of the clients on technical aspects of managing and realising the projects. There is no hard and fast rule. The basic brief is to support the teams and clients in any way that helps them to achieve successful implementation and to watch very carefully for any signs of sponsor or client abdication.

**Internal Coordinators and Facilitators**

We have already talked about most of the actions involved in setting up and running a Company Culture Change programme. What we have not talked about however is how to build in the learning aspect. We have created a number of project teams who will do the job what we need now is the learning component. In conventional action learning sets this taken care of by using professional facilitators who use the set meetings to focus the individual's learning needs. The problem here is that the project teams can meet at anytime and anywhere so it is not practical to use external facilitators.

We have tried a variety of solutions. In the early days we tried using self-management for the meetings and middle managers with simple training and ongoing support, as facilitators. This did not work very well, some middle managers were too busy and many either wanted to dominate or were not interested. We then tried self-management of the meetings with professional facilitators. This worked reasonably well but the timing of meetings was often difficult to arrange and it was costly. Finally we have adopted a model in which teams are responsible for both self-managing their meetings and self-managing their own facilitation with set members rotating through these roles on a meeting by meeting basis. Thus over the life of the set all members have the opportunity to be both meetings coordinator and facilitator. See our book on 'Empowering Change through Facilitation' for a detailed explanation of how this works.

Note. I personally believe that for the team members to both coordinate and facilitate themselves is in itself a valuable learning experience for all involved.

# Strengths and Weaknesses of In-Plant Programmes

*You can lead a horse to water but you can't make it drink.*

**Strengths**

In-Plant programmes deliver successful outcomes. They are cost effective, simple and reliable.

The learning lives on. Having run a programme with outside help management is able to adapt the process to its needs and continue it without further consultancy support

People are motivated by the experience. They are empowered; by being part of the decision making process and they will do extraordinary things like:

1. Working 1000 unpaid hours in the course of a twelve week project.
2. Spending a whole weekend making a video.
3. Working all night to be ready for a presentation.

It is ideal for doing things through people, rather than doing things to people. The process involves people; they become owners of the change they help to create.

Quicker often means slower; yes it takes time to be participative but in the long run it's quicker because what is implemented actually works.

By empowering people we are able to use all of the brains in the organisation not just a few large ones (Fujio Cho)
*'Involvement leads to ownership which creates commitment'*

There is always room for involvement. Even when the decision is inevitable it is always possible to have some influence over the 'how'

**Weaknesses**

These programmes are about change and change is very difficult. Many managers at all levels in organisations and particularly at the top are not comfortable with participation. They get to the top by being successful individuals not by being team players and because they don't like participation many don't like their people being participative either.

Some managers are afraid that they will be found wanting if cross functional teams are allowed to investigate what they are doing. They feel that problems in their areas of responsibility reflect badly on them not as things that need to be resolved for the good of the organisation.

Some managers feel threatened by the freedom the process gives to their people. As a result of the programme their people get to know their colleagues in other departments; meet and talk with the Chief Executive, visit other organisations to see how they tackle their problems et al.

Some team members will not wish to participate. Our experience shows that usually one or two people in each team will not be fully committed to the process; they miss meetings and contribute little but will always come to 'be seen' at the formal sessions!

A programme is only a programme no matter how good it is. Changing Company Culture is both a very effective means of introducing change and for demonstrating the value of empowerment. However to use it alone; as a one off to solve a specific problem can have very negative consequences. As Fred Herzberg said many years ago a '*goodie once given becomes a right*'. If you believe in participation, an In-Plant programme is a very good way to introduce it. If you don't, then it's probably better to stay with the traditional 'tell' style of management!

You could well lose senior people. Management teams often experience some trauma during the process for the reasons stated above. In the extreme some may decide to resign rather than continue. On one programme we had two of the senior managers resign, on another one person resigned and another changed jobs. On third occasion we had an all-night discussion during which some members of the management team tried to persuade the Chief Executive to abandon the programme because they felt it was too disruptive. To his eternal credit he stood firm.

So participation works and the benefits are enormous but it's like soup for breakfast, if you don't like, you don't like it. Can you learn to like it? Well look at Japan. One could argue that the Japanese are one of our most autocratic nations however they do participation very well as I found out in the early 80's when I started working there. It seems to me that if they can we can, if we value it enough!

# Case Studies

**Case 1** – Combining Supervisory and Organisational Development

One of the first In-Plant programmes we ran was with a major semiconductor manufacturer. The company decided that because they were planning to double the number of employees from 400 to 800 over the following six months, a training programme should be set up for the 24 supervisors. Conventional training programmes were considered and rejected as too theoretical for the level of the participants. The main goal of the training was to equip the existing supervisors to cope with the challenges inherent in the planned growth of the workforce. We offered an In-Plant programme using the expansion of the labour force as the source of the development projects, which was accepted. We started with a survey of the twenty-four supervisors and specialists who would be most affected by the changes which revealed that they felt there were four key issues that needed to be resolved to make the transition successful. These were:

1. The line stocking and materials supply systems
2. Communication within the plant
3. How the flexitime system was working
4. Morale and productivity

These were discussed and agreed with senior management and four of the senior team volunteered to become clients. We then ran an introductory workshop for the participants to provide them with some basic problem solving and team working skills. Participants were then given the opportunity to select the projects they would like to work on and four of the middle managers joined the teams as facilitators; these were supported by an external facilitator from Glasgow University. The programme ran for twelve weeks with the teams meeting weekly. Note. One of the teams estimated that it had worked 1000 man-hours on the project during the twelve-week period! Resulting benefits to the company included improved supervisory performance - and declines in both absenteeism and labour turnover. Absenteeism fell from 9% to 7.1%, and annual labour turnover from 10% to 7%. Recommendations from projects yielded valuable action, and a high level of enthusiasm was generated among the supervisors. Among benefits to individuals were greater awareness of the organisation and of the responsibilities of other areas; cross-fertilisation of ideas; improved self-confidence; enhanced motivation; deeper appreciation of their own and other people's problems; better management and supervisory abilities.

**Case 2** – Using the process with larger numbers

This is an example of a much larger scale programme in which we worked with a company in the North-East of England employing over 1,000 people in joinery manufacture. In the early 80's management decided to develop and run a supervisory training programme for its 72 supervisors. The business was in some trouble and the problem, as the company saw it, was that the supervisors were not performing effectively. They were not really identifying with the company and its objectives, and were therefore not handling the day-to-day problems, as management would have liked.

A Training Needs Analysis among the supervisory team showed that they were already well trained. Most had completed the National Examination Board in Supervisory Studies certificate, as well as many other courses: they obviously did not need further formal training. After some discussion with management, it was decided to focus on a motivational programme. This would use the Motorola model - a workshop plus a three-month In-Plant problem-solving programme. In this case, however, the problem-solving phase would focus on management development issues, and the introductory workshop would be extended to five days. It was also decided that, as the company was unionised, union representatives should be invited to participate.

Four introductory workshops were run over a three month period with all 72 supervisors attending. As part of the programme, participants were asked to write down what they felt 'stops you doing the best job you can'. The data was collected and collated for later use in identifying the stage two projects. On analysing the data it was immediately clear that the supervisors' views on the problems of improving productivity were very different to those of senior management. The supervisor's saw the problems as primarily 'managerial', and felt the real problem was that they were not allowed to manage. The initial objective of the programme had been, performance improvement through management development, but it was obvious from the feedback that the real problems were more complex. They were much more to do with the way the organisation was being managed than with the managing skills of middle and first-line management.

At about this time the Managing Director changed. The new Managing Director was an old 'Company' man brought back in to sort out the production problems. In discussion with him it was agreed that we should change the focus of the programme, moving from management development to organisational development. It was agreed that we would use the problems identified in the workshops as the basis for the performance improvement projects. Initially eleven projects were identified, a twelfth (on cash flow) being added later. The original eleven were:

Communication - Examine existing channels of company communication and comment on their effectiveness. What improvements can be made?

Customer Service - Evaluate current levels of customer service in terms of quality and delivery, and recommend a means of achieving improvement.

Computer Planning Systems - Examine the existing computer-based system as an aid to production management, and assess their value; and what training should be given to the personnel involved.

Absenteeism - Examine the cause and effects of absenteeism in the company and suggest how this could be reduced.

Maintenance - Examine the operation of the maintenance department and make recommendations for improving the present cost/benefit ratio.

Operator Training - Investigate the company's approach to training with a view to improving labour efficiency and suggest how this can be integrated with other methods of increasing productivity.

Distribution Costs - Examine the increasing costs of distribution, and consider how this could be reduced.

Stock Control - Materials account for almost 50% of the company's cost.  How could this be reduced?

Product Development - Examine the company's existing product range, and recommend developments which would utilise company strengths and maximise profitability.

Application of Microprocessors - Analyse present work situations, and identify potential applications for microprocessors.

Value of the Programme - Investigate the transfer of skills and knowledge acquired on the supervisory training aspect of the course to the daily working environment of the participants, and determine the effectiveness of first-line management in their day-to-day jobs.

The change in emphasis was greeted with enthusiasm by the supervisors who agreed to form eleven project teams to tackle the problems. The In-Plant phase finally got underway six months after the programme began. The senior managers took the client role with middle managers acting as facilitators, the consultants as external advisers, with the Personal Manager as the internal coordinator.  In addition we contracted two people from Teesside Polytechnic to work with the teams in the early stages. Changing the focus of the programme from management development to direct concern with solving specific problems had a considerable impact on the motivation of the teams.  They seemed to develop and grow with the challenge of being able to do something about their problems. Three months later, when the programme was reviewed, most teams had produced worthwhile results:

The customer service project identified a need for a specific progress chaser, as well as a computer VDU system, which was later installed.

The computer project concluded that, in fact, the current computer system was really working well and the final paragraph of their report said 'in conclusion, we consider that, contrary to initial expectations, the computer and the plans which it produces are almost always correct. Errors, where they occur, are due to misinterpretation of the printout. It is felt that adequate explanation of the system must be given to new operatives before they are asked to work off these plans.'

The team looking into absenteeism found that one of the main causes of absenteeism was lack of interest and motivation in the work force. They recommended a number of changes in working practices, including the introduction of a self-financing attendance incentive scheme linked to production dispatches (as was the staff bonus scheme at that time), and the introduction of a scheme to generate interest among the work force by giving them more information about the destination of products.

The maintenance project team reported on a number of problems, including the lack of preventive maintenance, the call-out system, and especially, the management of the maintenance function. They recommended that the maintenance team should actually be set up and funded as a service department. They also recommended that they should be involved in the selection and purchase of capital equipment, as they would be required to maintain such equipment at a later date.

Operator Training - this team found that there was no overall policy for training charge-hands or operators and personnel training records, whilst available, were difficult to access. They recommended changes in these three areas. In addition, they recognised the motivational value of training and felt that a greater involvement with the union in developing training programmes and better cross training and understanding of other roles would increase motivation, and therefore performance.

Distribution Costs - the team made a number of round routing changes, improvements in route and load planning, greater use of the computer in building loads, and a recommendation to increase the number of merchants, so that small drops could be used through these outlets. They recommended that the company investigate a change in the type of vehicle in use to something which would be easier to load and unload, and produced figures to support their contention.

The team examining potential reductions in the cost of raw materials learned that the raw material budget for the current year would be £9.2m, and that to April, when some £2m had already been spent, only £400 in cash discounts had been obtained. They recommended a more effective use of off-cuts, better material utilisation - which they estimated would save £28,000 in a full year. As far as improvements in quality control were concerned, the team identified possible savings of some £30,000. Their final recommendations included the appointment of a Materials Manager, who they estimated could make a saving of £92,000 in a full year, based on the previous year's costs.

The new products team looked at three areas: the introduction of new products; an examination of the present utilisation of labour, machinery methods and space; and a consideration of the development and assembly of by-products of waste and reject materials. This team actually developed a new model door using spare material on the site, which they felt met the market need for any interior location. It would be easy to make and cheaper than the existing product. By the time of the presentation this was fully developed and costed.

Microprocessors - this team identify a number of opportunities for using microprocessors. The first was for a microprocessor in the kilns, which would facilitate a much more efficient through-put at a cost of £2,500; a computer to x-cut components, which at a cost of £12,000 would save two jobs; a microprocessor in the saw shop, which would enable the saw doctor to do two jobs at once, thus reducing through-put time by 50%; and a microprocessor costing about £1,000 for the stock control system in the maintenance stores, which they felt could help with the tracking of the 10,000 items worth about £170,000 in the maintenance stores at that time. They further recommended the use of personal computers as word processors and for other office tasks. One of the main values of the project to this team was to develop a greater understanding of microprocessors, their operation and applications.

Skills Transfer - the team used a questionnaire-based approach to see how people felt the skills developed on the programme could be applied in practice. This revealed that the programme had helped in a number of ways:

1.  Enabling managers and supervisors to understand each other's problems had been of great benefit to those involved, and through them, to the company.

2.  An enhanced awareness of the need for good communication had been highlighted, and this had actually improved during the course of the programme. However, there was need for further work on this by senior management.

3.  The skills and knowledge learnt from the course, particularly the problem-solving aspects, had been extremely useful.

4.  The opportunity the course provided to understand and value the talents of others had been very valuable both to individuals and the company.

 When it came to determining the effectiveness of the programme for the supervisors however, many felt that whilst some positive results had been achieved, the attitudes of their bosses had changed little, and most were still being managed in an authoritarian way.

The cash flow project. This was not one of the original projects but was introduced by the Managing Director at an early stage in the programme. The team working on this were asked to identify specific areas where cash could be released into the business, and proved to be highly successful. By April, it had actually released some £620,000 into the system, thus improving the cash flow by that amount.

A plenary review with all involved was held in the April. There was consensus that the process had been extremely valuable and that it should continue. It was decided to take what had been learnt about the problem solving process in the first programme, and adapt the approach as an ongoing way of solving specific business problems. It was agreed that some of the participants of the original programme would become clients and advisers, and people directly involved in the problems, including shop-floor workers would work in the problem solving teams.

A second programme was launched in the latter half of that year with six teams of ten people working on major problems selected by management. The main project was concerned with the reorganisation of the factory (2). By then the market was in severe decline and competition had increased; there was a real need for enhanced manufacturing efficiency. The team responsible for this project developed a new manufacturing layout, presented it to management, implemented the plan and negotiated 150 redundancies. All this was carried out between September and early January. The team actually supervised the changeover of the factory during the Christmas shut-down period.

The following June the company again reorganised and the MD retired. This brought about a shift in policy at the top, with the new MD deciding to fall back on more traditional management methods to run the business. This meant that there was no further development of the programme, although problem-solving teams were subsequently used to look at a number of issues. Five years later the company was taken over by a Swedish competitor.

**Case 3** – Joint Management / Union Programme

This programme had its beginnings in a joint union/ management training programme organised by the main Trades Union. During the course participants highlighted a number of issues, things which were stopping them doing a good job. They asked the management during the course review for permission to try and solve some of these problems. The management team agreed and we were asked to organise the programme.

The discussions about this programme coincided with a need the company had already identified, to solve a specific problem in the newly commissioned printed circuit board manufacturing plant. The symptoms of this were the inability of the unit to produce consistently, both volume and quality. It was possible to achieve 90% volume at 70% quality or 70% volume at 90% quality but not both of the higher figures at the same time. An audit showed that those involved felt the problems were largely attitudinal. After some discussion management agreed that the issues were similar to those highlighted by those who had attended the joint union / management course. If the In-Plant approach was right for the one situation, it must be right for the other. Management decided to set up an In-Plant programme with people in the printed circuit board plant.

It was decided to run two programmes in parallel. The first for the team who had been on the joint union/management training programme, they would work on three issues identified during the course. The second was for the printed board plant people and was designed to provide them with the opportunity to solve their own problems.

The Union/management team programme was launched with three projects: redeployment, Industrial Relations and attitudes (rather than communication). There were seven people in each project team. Three senior managers acted as clients and one member from each team, as facilitators. The report-back stage of the project was reached at the end of November and the first phase of implementation complete by April the following year. Two of these teams functioned well and implemented their recommendations with the full support of their clients. The third team had considerable difficulties with the project, due both to problems in the team and lack of support from the client. The team did solve its internal problems in the end, and made a valuable contribution to the overall project.

The PCB programme started with a Problem-Identification workshop, which was run twice over two consecutive weekends. All supervision, management and specialist functions in the PCB area (over 40 people in total) attended. The weekend sessions were designed to identify the major problems facing participants in improving the performance of the plant, to generate a need to solve them and to encourage a team working.

The next stage was a Project Definition workshop for senior management. This was also run residentially over a weekend and had three objectives:

1.  To develop a realisation amongst management that they were part of the problem;

2.  To enable senior managers to identify the problems which naturally belonged to them and to agree the projects on which the teams would work;

3.  To gain the commitment of the management team to solving the problems

The large amount of data collected at the Problem-Identification workshops on the PCB plant problems, was presented to senior management. They were asked to discuss the issues raised, to see if they agreed with them, and to identify what 'belonged to them'. The problems were gradually refined into six main projects.

This was a particularly interesting workshop and raised a number of issues:

Firstly, there was a high level of concern that the feedback and indeed the session itself was a direct reflection on the ability of some of the managers present. They felt the whole process implied that they were not doing their jobs properly, and if they were to accept this it would weaken their position.

Secondly, there was a lot of concern that to use the people in the organisation to actually solve what they saw as 'management' problems might in some way undermine the managers' authority.

Thirdly, there was a great deal of fear of looking foolish in front of colleagues, and strong concern not to be exposed.

The meeting started well, with some fairly open discussion on the points, which had been raised. While there was some defensiveness (expressions like "they don't understand" were used), most people thought it was fairly harmless. However, as the implications in terms of commitment and management involvement necessary to make the programme work became clear, concerns started to build. At some stage after dinner there were a number of pleas to go home and forget about the whole thing. However, the Managing Director stood firm, and by a little after midnight we emerged with an agreement to go ahead with six major project areas, which encompassed much of the data collected from the supervisory team.

The next step was for the clients to write up their projects linking in with the collected data, in preparation for the project launch. In addition, it was agreed that those managers who were not clients, would be offered as project advisers. This latter decision was made to ensure that all senior managers were involved in the projects. This meant that management gained a 'hands-on' appreciation of how the teams felt, and how effective they were at solving problems. It also served to increase senior management's sense of ownership of the solutions produced.

The project teams, started work in October. The teams themselves worked well, but as with the Switchgear programme we had some problems with the facilitators (all middle managers). Some were always too busy to attend the team meetings, others wanted to take charge. Luckily this did not seem to seriously affect the teams' performance. The recommendations were presented in February, and were well received by senior management.

In the client team meeting which followed most clients had identified some valuable actions from the reports both for themselves and for the teams. Some of the clients however, saw the further involvement of the team as more of a problem than an opportunity. For example one client, whilst accepting the recommendations of the project team should be implemented said he did not want them involved in the implementation. A considerable amount of time was spent in discussing this whole issue, and a number of arguments why they should not be involved were put forward, including lack of expertise. Little credence was given to the fact that the project team had been able to harness the necessary expertise to analyse the problems, present the recommendations and argue the case for them.

Only three teams went on to implement their findings. The recommendations of the other three, particularly the pre-production and engineering teams proved too politically sensitive, and nothing was done. As for the quality project, which was the crux of the original problem, the team found that the major cause of the quality problems lay in the reward systems. The operators were paid through a conventional piece-work system taken from another part of the factory. This rewarded the operators for the volume of production rather than for its quality. The project team recommended that this should be changed to a team bonus scheme based on both volume and quality. In addition, they made a number of specific technical recommendations designed to make achievement of quality easier. The main recommendations were implemented and proved successful.

In addition to these two programmes, a further third programme was started in the following spring. This involved participants from a second joint Union/management course and had two projects - materials control and shortages. The project teams reported back in May and the recommendations were accepted and implemented.

# Creating Your Own In-Plant Programmes

These notes are offered to help readers who would like to create and run their own Changing Company Culture programmes. We hope you will find them useful.

**Designing the programme**

In-Plant programmes are a vehicle for delivering change through participation; empowering the people to create their own change. It's about getting 'buy in' to deliver a change that will have significant impact on part or the whole of the organisation. It's not for simple changes like introducing new software for the computers or new procedure for writing monthly reports. These are what we call 'closed' ended problems. There is one 'right answer' which most people will see as logical. If on the other hand the change involves the way people work together, productivity, customer care, flexi working hours etc., these are 'open' ended problems. There are a variety of possible answers; any one of which will work if the people who must make it happen own the chosen solution. Equally, if the organisation uses annual attitude surveys the 'open ended' problems identified by such surveys make ideal projects for Changing Company Culture programmes and have the advantage that as there is a survey every year so there will be an opportunity to embed the process. Note. See our publication on Problem Solving and Decision Making for a more detailed explanation about open and closed ended problems.

However you do it the first step in the process is to create 'buy in' in order to get recognition of the need and thus commitment. What you want to do needs to be based on facts and these facts need to be 'recognised' by those who will be affected as something that needs to be done which means that it needs to come from those who will be involved. There many ways of doing this; you can use Attitude Surveys, specific data gathering, performance statistics etc.

The data then needs to be analysed to highlight key issues. See the following example:

ISSUE 1 - The recruitment of good young people into the business - there is a serious lack of personal communication skills. They are only able to relate to computers, not people. Too computer-driven, need more team building. The education system is at fault - it lays emphasis on gaining degrees. No one wants to be a craftsman anymore and this is killing off the construction industry.

ISSUE 2 - Senior employees no longer want to move up the professional ladder. They are quite happy to settle back and stay where they are though we've put a lot of effort and time into them but we are not getting the return we would like.

ISSUE 3 - We are a large organisation and it is difficult to get everyone working along the same lines and towards the same goals. It is also difficult to make sure we stay in line with all the new legislation - there seems to be so much of it.

ISSUE 4 - Keeping up with the amount of training necessary. At the moment we are driven by necessity rather than by desire to improve the workforce. We don't have a centralised training philosophy, what we do is all very ad hoc.

ISSUE 5 - Ongoing people development; skill shortages in production and development, IT design and software development. Training of apprentices is difficult as young people are generally unskilled.

These issues are all 'open' ended; there are no right answers they are thus ideal for Action Learning projects.

The next step is to discuss issues with senior management to see firstly if they agree that these are real problems and if they do, to propose the idea of an In-Plant programme to resolve them. This means describing the In-Plant methodology and tabling an outline programme setting out how it would work, the number of projects, clients, teams (how many and who should be involved) etc., see annex A for example programme. If management accept the proposal the next step is to formalise the programme, choose clients and write TOR's, agree details of participation and invite all involved to the launch.

**Writing Terms of Reference**

If management like the idea and agree to go ahead the next thing is to decide who in the senior team will be the client for which issue? Once this has been agreed the clients can be helped to write Terms of Reference for their projects, see example below.

---

**PROJECT TERMS OF REFERENCE**

**Title:** Adopting consistent working practices

**Client: -** William Burns, Operations Director

**Current Situation:** The following issue has been raised in the annual Attitude Survey

We are a large organisation and it is difficult to get everyone working along the same lines and towards the same goals. It is also difficult to make sure we stay in line with all the new legislation - there seems to be so much of it.

**Activities:** I would like the team to:

Conduct a survey to evaluate working practices in the various parts of our organisation. I am specifically interested to know if a) we have

---

consistent practices across the organisation and b) whether we are working in line with the legislation.

Identify similar organisations, there are two or three in our region and visit them to benchmark our current practices.

Recommend what needs to be consistent, like Health and Safety practices and customer care for example, where there are short falls and make proposals on where we need to improve

**Expected Outcomes:** A report to be presented in the plenary session on 19th December setting out your findings and recommendations.

## The Launch Meeting

The basic rule is that all of those who will work on the projects need to be invited to the launch meeting. In the case of our example the Annual Attitude Survey involved all employees, over 1000+ people. We could not have all of these working on five projects so the first decision was that there would be a number of plenary meetings to which everyone would be invited and where the Chief Executive and his team would communicate the results of the survey and the actions proposed including the setting up of the five teams.

The issue then was how to form the teams. There are really two options, to ask for volunteers during the plenary presentations or to select for example supervisors and workers representatives. The key advantage of selection is that management can use the development opportunity to meet specific needs.

In this case those who would participate in the teams were then invited to a plenary session for briefing. This was held in the evening and had an informal tone, starting with a buffet and ending with drinks. The Chief Executive made the opening presentation and chaired the meeting. The consultant then explained the In-Plant concept and the structure of the programme. The clients then present their projects, which were written up on flip charts pinned up around the room as they presented. When all of the projects have been presented the consultant explains that people could now choose the projects they would like to work on and that once this was done they could adjourn to the bar!

## Getting Started

This is normally done with a half-day workshop where participants are introduced to the concept of working in problem solving teams using the methodology set out in our Changing Company Culture Teams, Participants Guide. This explains the process, provides information on coordinating team meetings, facilitating the learning and some of the basic problem solving tools the teams will need in the investigation phase.

Workshops normally start with a general introduction:

*Your task over the next three months is to investigate the problem set but your client and produce recommendations on what should be done about it. This investigation will involve you in studying the current situation within the plant and also identifying and reviewing 'best practice'. We suggest that you hold team meetings every two weeks. When, is up to you, but if you would like to meet during lunch time, HR will be happy to arrange sandwiches and coffee.*

*You will be responsible for both managing your meetings and facilitating your own learning. We recommend that you rotate through these roles on a meeting by meeting basis so that over during the three months all team members will have the opportunity to be both meetings coordinator and facilitator.*

Note. For more detailed information on facilitating see our book on 'Facilitating Action Learning Teams'

Participants are then introduced to the concept of team working and the Coordinator and facilitator roles using a number of short problem solving and decision making exercises. The workshop concludes with the first team meetings at which the teams are encouraged to create their work plan for the project, to agree initial actions and the date of the next meeting.

**Investigation and Recommendations Phase**

Participants use the In-Plant Action Learning - Participants Guide to lead them through the Investigation and Recommendation Phase. This, essentially practical process, it provides teams with a framework for what they have to do in the allotted timescale, a common language for working together and a structure for keeping the team on track. The consultant monitors the progress of the teams and if there are real difficulties, which in my experience are very rare, the client can be asked to arrange a meeting with the team to review progress, extra people can be added and HR can be asked to provide support.

**Presentation and Feedback**

From the consultant's stand point this is an important milestone so it's worth spending time with the teams to review the reports and go through the presentations with them before the event. Try to ensure that all members of the team have a part to play during the presentation process even if it's only changing the slides. It's worth managing the order of the presentations, start and finish with a good one and put the weaker ones in the middle and it is also important to make sure that each presentation is followed by questions, even if they are asked by the consultant. Finally no presentation should be accepted or rejected on the night; the team have worked for three months to produce their recommendations, they at least deserve to be given serious consideration. The meeting should close with a 'Thank You' from the CEO and the promise of a quick response.

The consultant should attend the client team meeting where the projects are considered to ensure that as far as possible the response will be objective and the recommendations that are accepted for implementation by the teams are 'real' and worthwhile. Once these have been agreed the clients will be asked to write new TOR's, which should be reviewed by the consultant and the management team prior to the presentation to the teams. Note. It is important to stress the change of client role at this stage. The client now becomes the project manager and the team work with him/her to implement the desired solution. See briefing note

## Implementation Phase

In this phase the role of the consultant is more one of support, enabling and encouraging the teams to do a good job. There will now be regular meetings with the client to report progress and new members with specialist skills may be recruited to help with the implementation. This is now a 'real' time activity and the client is responsible for its success. This is also where the real cultural change takes place; changing relationships, adopting new working practices, working cross functionally etc. It is therefore very important that the consultant monitor this process and flag any evidence of 'back sliding' on the part of client's, see case 3, with the sponsor!

## Review and Evaluation

This is normally held about three months after the start of the Implementation phase. Some teams may have finished their project whilst others have some way to go. The aim of this meeting is:

1.  To recognise the work that the teams have done over the previous six months, much of it in their own time and to say 'thanks'.
2.  To review the achievements, what has gone well and the areas where things might have been improved
3.  To evaluate the process. Has participative problem solving helped organisation to be more effective. If so, how can the philosophy be incorporate into the future modus operandi of the organisation?

The review session is normally run by the participants themselves and involves all clients, facilitators and anyone else who has been part of the programme. The primary objective is to review the programme and evaluate its benefits. What objectives were achieved, what were not and why? It is an opportunity for all involved to share their views about the experience to see what has been learnt from it. Such sessions are usually very open; success and failure are discussed with equal candour, both being seen as providing a learning opportunity.

## Conclusions

There are no simple 'right' answers to what makes In-Plant programmes succeed or fail. Our experience, having developed and worked with the model now for over thirty years, says that if you have the right sponsor, the commitment of senior management, the right planning at the start and find a good site coordinator the process works. Hopefully the organisation has learnt a more effective way of managing its open ended problems and will incorporate what it has learnt into its managing philosophy and extended the process of the programme to involve everyone. We have had programmes, which cascaded down to work force and unions with middle managers becoming clients to working teams. In the Semiconductor example the process of team problem solving became institutionalised with multi-level, cross functional teams solving complex, many faceted problems as a feature of everyday life. In a large Electronics company the process is used whether complex cross-functional problems are encountered with past participants becoming clients and facilitators.

Each programme is unique because each organisation is unique and the way it is carried forward is a decision that each organisation must make for itself. The key thing to remember is that we need all on the brains in our organisations, not just the few big ones at the top and the only way of harnessing them is through participation and empowerment. If we can be of any further help please do not hesitate to contact us.

George Boulden, November 2014

### Annex A - Example In-Plant Programmes

## STRATEGIC TASK FORCE ACTION LEARNING PROJECT

Introduction

This proposal sets out the framework for the *Strategic Task Force* Action Learning project.

The program will run in five stages;

Stage 1 - Five-day launch workshop   February 18 to 22

Stage 2 - Six-week information-gathering phase during which participants return to work to explore resources and collect relevant information.

Stage 3 - Three-day mid-project workshop, venue and dates to be agreed, which provides the opportunity for participants to share what they have done and agree the next steps in the project.

Stage 4 - Second six-week phase during which participants return home and work to assess potential solutions.

Stage 5 - Provides the opportunity for participants to meet, agree findings, and complete a formal report. To conclude, a formal presentation with recommendations will be made to senior management.

Objectives

To provide a practical solution to the client's problem
To develop participants interpersonal, problem solving and team working skills

For

***Strategic Task Force*** team members, clients and sponsor

***Method*** – All Stages

The Action Learning approach will be used throughout. This is based on three guiding principles:

1.  Human beings learn best from reflected practice.
2.  The best test of any learning is trying it out in action.
3.  The process of learning is greatly strengthened by regularly sharing the experience with others who are also learning by doing.

Outline Program

Stage 1 - Introductory Workshop - 18/22nd February
Stage 2 - Investigation – Feb to March
Stage 3 - Interim Review Meeting – Early April – Venue to be agreed
Stage 4 - Test Recommendations and Benchmark – Mid April to May
Stage 5 - Presentation and Recommendations to senior managers and the Senior Executive Team – May   - final dates to be confirmed.

Introductory Workshop – 18/22nd February

This workshop is designed to launch the ***Task Force*** program.  The focus is on building participants into a team, providing them with some common problem solving tools and producing an agreed action plan for the project.

Objectives

To develop participants into a team
To develop understanding of the project and agree roles, responsibilities and the communication structure

Content

Introduction to Action Learning
Strategic Task Forces
Clarify project objectives, goals
Tools of team working – how the team will work
Identification of resources for project – local, regional, global
Facilitating learning – sharing knowledge and expertise
Characteristics of effective teams
Nature & Process of Change
Project management – how the project will be managed
Personal development and learning objectives
Japanese culture and its impact on business
The financial services industry in Japan
Identify next steps

Interim Review Meeting – Mid-March

Introduction

This second workshop is designed to review the status of the project and identify outstanding issues and tasks. It also provides the opportunity to focus the learning and to plan the next phase of the project.

Objectives

To review what has been addressed and what is outstanding
To review the effectiveness of the team working
To review 'lessons learned' from Stage 1 of project

Expected outcomes

It is expected that by the end of the second workshop participants will have:-

A clear picture of where they are in the project and what they need to do to completion
Undertaken a realistic appraisal of the project
Had the opportunity to share their learning
Agreed the next steps

Final Workshop / Presentation of Recommendations – May

Introduction

In this final workshop the team will consolidate their findings, complete the analysis of data, prepare a report and present their findings and recommendations to the client. Learning from the project will be reviewed and the program and process evaluated.

Objectives

To enable participants to present their findings and recommendations to the client and his team
To provide the opportunity to present the findings to the senior management team in Philadelphia.
To share personal development experiences and review the benefits of the program

Expected outcomes

It is expected that by the end of the workshop:-

Participants will have made a convincing presentation of their findings and recommendations to the client
The client will have a clear set of actionable recommendations that will enable the business challenge to be addressed
Participants would have honed their interpersonal, team working and problem solving skills
Participants would have established an ongoing high impact collaborative and cross functional network

**Programme Template**

# Action Learning Programme for XXX

Prepared by:

Prepared for:

Date:

Contents:

Introduction

Objectives

For

Method

Programme

Budget

# Further Reading

If you have found reading this book interesting you may also find the following useful.

1.  For an insight into human behaviour I recommend Dr. Thomas A. Harris is the author of *I'm OK – You're OK*, the 1969 bestseller based upon the ideas of Transactional Analysis by <u>Dr Eric Berne</u>. ISBN 0-06-072427. If you find this interesting you may also like to read 'The Games People Play, by Dr Eric Berne ISBN 0-345-41003-3

2.  In the same géndre but more focused on 'rapport' skills is NPL, How to Build a Successful Life by Richard Brandler, Alessio Roberti & Owen Fitzpatrick, published by Harper Collins, ISBN 978-0-00-749741-6

3.  For a deeper understanding of values I suggest 'What Matters Most' by Hyrum W Smith, published by Franklin Covey Co. ISBN 0-684-87256-0

4.  For an entertaining insight into the real world of influencing I recommend the book 'When I Stop Talking You'll Know I'm Dead by Jerry Weintraub, Rich Cohen and George Clooney, Published by Hachette Books ISBN 978-0-446-54815-1

5.  To learn more about 'action learning' I recommend Reg's original book on the subject 'The ABC of Action Learning' Published by Gower Publications, ISBN 978-1-4094-2703-2. Mike Pedlar's Action Learning in Practice, Third Edition, Ed Mike Pedler, Gower Press, ISBN 0 566 07795 7 and More than Management Development, Edited by David Casey & David Pearce, Gower Press, 1977. ISBN 0-566-022005-X This book reviews the early GEC programmes referred to in this text.

6.  If you would like to learn more about Facilitation then 'Facilitating Action Learning: A Practitioner's Guide' by <u>Mike Pedler</u> and <u>Christine Abbott</u> is a useful read. Also

David Casey's excellent paper on The Emerging Role of the Set Advisers, copies available from ALA International

## Books George has written on Action Learning and related topics

The following books are published by ALA International. They are available on our web site www.ala-international.com and from **Google Books** and **Amazon** in Epub or paperback formats.

## Books about Action learning

Applications of Action Learning – describes the philosophy of action learning and its applications. ISBN 978-0-9560822-4-4

Own Job Action Learning – describes how Action learning can be used in individual development programmes. ISBN 978-0-9560822-0-6

In-Plant Action Learning – This book explains how the philosophy of Action learning can be used to deliver organisational change. ISBN 978-0-9560822-3-7

In-Plant Action Learning - Participants Guide – This Guide is designed to help In-Plant teams to self-manage and facilitate their own learning; available from ALA International.

Empowering Change Through Facilitation – describes how the process of facilitation is used to develop participants in Action Learning sets.  ISBN 978-0 -9560822-9-9

## Books about Personal Development

Managers as Leaders - This book show how management and leadership combine to ensure the effective delivery of the task. ISBN 978-0-9560822-2-0

Managing Difficult Relationships – examines the reasons for difficult relationships and provides a 'framework' for negotiating win / win solutions. ISBN 978-0-9560822-5-1

Change; Become a Winner - I believe that life is not a rehearsal, it's a journey and you can change it. If you would like to do something different with your life this book is for you. ISBN 13 978-1503185401, ISBN 10:1503185400

Values & Style; the Key to Productivity –The common denominator in performance improvement in organizations, is managing style. The things that stop people doing the best job they can stem from 'them and us' attitudes. These are based on cultural values and determine the way human beings perceive their roles and relationships within hierarchies. This book explores the nature of values and style and how they impact the operating effectiveness of organizations and societies. (Under Review)

Re-Engineering the Workplace – This book describes the Japanese approach to productivity with practical examples on how it can be applied in practice.

**Useful web sites for Action Learning**

Action Learning is a worldwide network. The following are some useful contacts in the Action Learning world:-

The International Foundation for Action Learning (IFAL), formally The Action Learning Trust www.ifal.org.uk

International Community of Action Learners (ICAL). This is a loose federation of Action Learning practitioners. Their web site can be found on www.tlainc.com

IMC acts as a clearing house for academic institutions offering Action Learning programmes. Contact www.imc.org.uk/imcal-inter For articles www.free-press.com/journals/gaja

The Revans Library at Salford University www.salford.ac.uk

World Institute for Action Learning, www.wial.com

**Please use the following link to find our books on Amazon.**

http://www.amazon.com/s?ie=UTF8&page=1&rh=n%3A283155%2Cp_27%3AGeorge%20Boulden

I will be very grateful if you will take a few minutes to write a review on this book while you are here. Thank you.

George Boulden

www.ingramcontent.com/pod-product-compliance
Lightning Source LLC
Chambersburg PA
CBHW070946210326
41520CB00021B/7074